The Crow That Couldn't Fly

Donte Hayes

ISBN 979-8-89383-065-1

Now this wasn't your ordinary crow!
This crow was a lot larger than the rest.
His chest and head were always held high and his tail feathers hung a tad bit lower than normal to the ground, somewhat distorted in a way, but to his advantage, this all worked in his favor.

This made his balance impeccable and all of the other crows were actually pretty inferior when this crow came around.

To be honest, I actually think that the other crows were scared of him.

They would fly circles around him gawking loudly and even
taunting the crow by dropping
sticks and rocks out of the air or high trees.

But, of all things, this one crow could not fly!!!! I mean he maybe could get about 2-3 feet off the ground with a jump and a couple of flaps of that one disabled wing of his.

On this one Saturday morning, the crow was awake early with the sun, as usual, taking his morning walk so he could get all the worms as the early bird does.
Along his morning stroll, he spotted a half-eaten sandwich lying in the street.

The sun was beaming brightly on this day,
so he knew that he had to move quickly.

Between that sandwich baking on the hot pavement and the other crows nearby already plotting on it, the crow Homie knew that he had to act fast.

He took off flapping and skipping with
his eyes on that sandwich. He just knew
that this could be his only meal of the day.
He ran so fast that he merely overran the meal.

The other on-looking crows all thought he had blown it, but the crow Homie was skipping with a little more Pizzaz as if he had somewhere to go.
He knew that if he reached the fence, he would be able to jump, skip and flap his way up to the top of the fence, which was just a jump away from the elementary school's balcony, where he would be safe from the other crows.

By now, it is pretty obvious to notice that this sandwich had missing pieces. The crow Homie was able to snatch him a real good meal along the way. All that was left was a piece of cheese and a slice of bread.

The other crows are really mad now. They also knew that he could not fly and that there was only one way to safety: the fence.

The gang of crows must've gotten smart, because, one by one, the crows took off flying towards the balcony in wishes of cutting him off.
Still running to his spot, the crow Homie noticed the change In the plot of tho other crows.

Therefore, his plans changed. On his way to the gate, he noticed a hawk circling and screeching in the midst. This is bad for all of them.

The crow Homie slows down to not be such a moving target for the hawk. Still with food in his mouth, he still decides to keep heading towards that fence. As he reaches the bottom of the fence, he sizes it up and gets ready to make his next move.

All of the other crows were wondering what could be taking so long. Usually, the crow would've made it up that fence by now. Not paying any mind to the hawk in the air, the gang of crows peeked out from underneath the balcony's ledge to get a better view of the crow Homie.

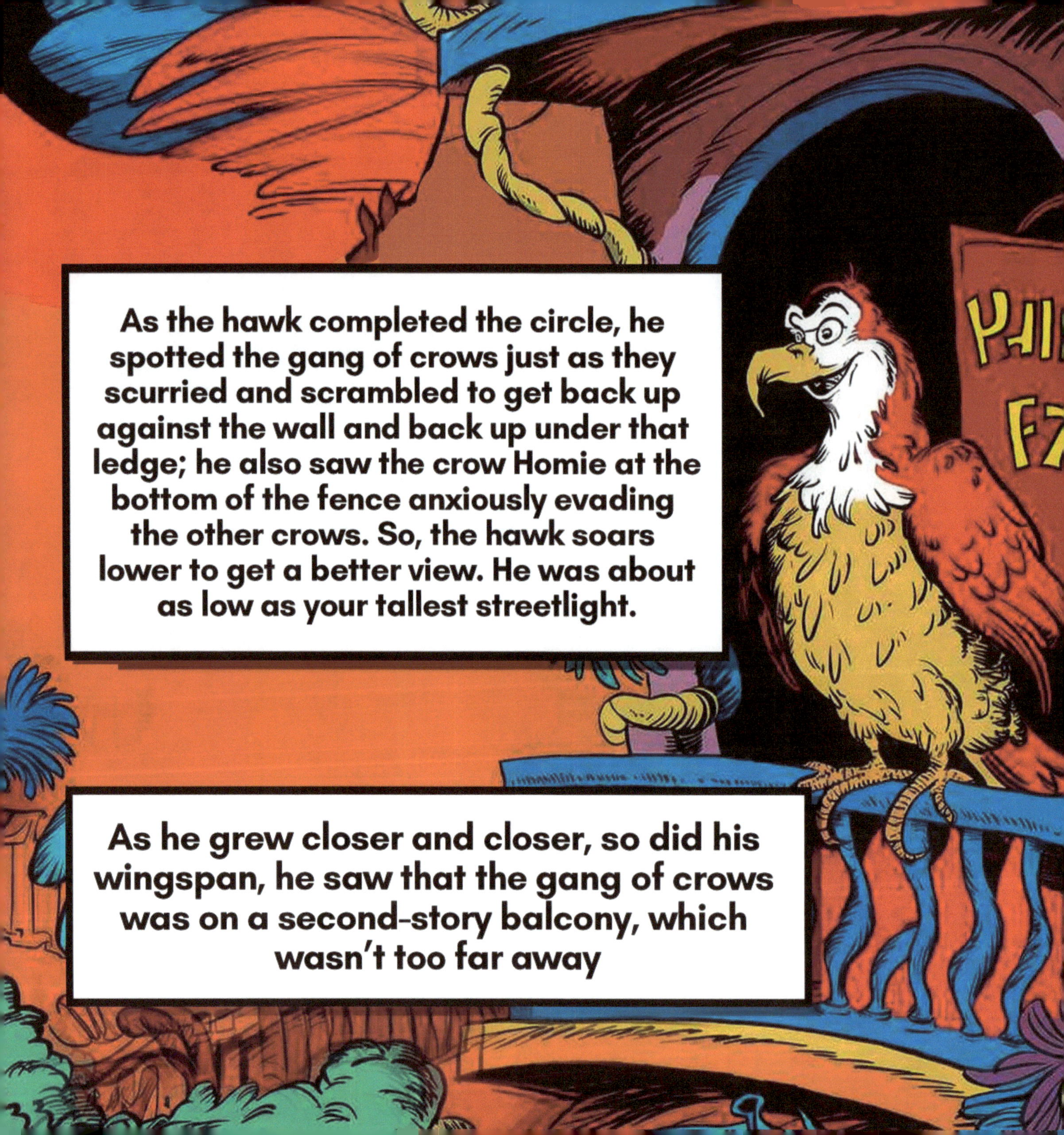
As the hawk completed the circle, he spotted the gang of crows just as they scurried and scrambled to get back up against the wall and back up under that ledge; he also saw the crow Homie at the bottom of the fence anxiously evading the other crows. So, the hawk soars lower to get a better view. He was about as low as your tallest streetlight.

As he grew closer and closer, so did his wingspan, he saw that the gang of crows was on a second-story balcony, which wasn't too far away

Apparently, the gang figured that it was time to go. Leaving the crow Homie behind, the entire flock of crows took off flying in the opposite direction of the hawk.
The crow Homie noticed that the gang had left the territory, so he made his move up that fence and onto the now clear balcony level.

The hawk was still screeching and circling even lower and louder now, wondering why this one crow did not fly away.
Instead, the crow Homie just jumped as high as he could, flapping but continuously going down slowly and all of the others just thought that they had witnessed the crow's demise.

The hawk and the crow were both on the balcony by now, about ten feet away from each other. That's when the hawk notices this wasn't an ordinary crow.
This one crow could not fly.

As they stood just about at eye level with one another, the hawk stepped forward to take a closer look at the crow, which also, at the same time the hawk whipped his wings open to his full wingspan, revealing its beautiful pattern of war wounds.

The crow stood there intimidated, but admiring this beautiful view. Usually, if a bird was to have this view of this majestic sequence, it was to be their last beautiful moment, better known as The Kiss of Death.

Frantically, the flock of crows flew overhead, noisily awaiting the fate of the standoff on the balcony.

Obviously, the hawk stood a lot larger and stronger, but the crow Homie could easily tell that this too was also a wounded warrior, or the hawk was also labeled as an outcast by a flock of birds, because of his injuries.

So, as a sign of respect, the hawk took an exhale to lower his chest and that's when the crow Homie slowly raised his wings, revealing the one partially paralyzed wing of his.

The hawk turned his head to acknowledge the army of crows, walked towards the trickling edge of the balcony and let out a loud screech in the air.

I guess, as a warning to the flock, because after that, the hawk turns towards the crow Homie signaling for him to join the podium.

The crow waits for a minute, then with a boost of confidence, he flaps and skips to the edge as well. Now the hawk and the crowd stood side by side, opposing the army of crows.
As the thunderstorms were brewing, the intensity grew stronger. A bolt of lightning strikes on the valley floor in between the standoff.

The hawk knew that it was time, because he turned to the crow and gave this look to say let's do this. Not knowing what he was getting himself into, the crow just felt that he could trust this hawk,so he shrugs in agreement.

Another powerful lightning strikes the rooftop causing the flying flock of crows to swarm in their direction.
Noticing, but hardly budging, the hawk calmly just spread his wings. Nervously, the crow panicked as he awaited the approaching swarm. The swarm finally reaches the crow, giving him a lift-off.

During the swarm, the hawk could notice that the crow Homie was struggling to fly, flipping, and flapping through the air. Meanwhile, the hawk just soared with the swarm. The crow stopped flipping, but still flapping for his life.

Just as they begin to descend, the hawk flaps his wings and blows a strong gust of wind towardthe crow, causing him to open his wings and stop flipping.
Another gust of wind blew, there was a little turbulence, but with him paying so much attention to the hawk.

Finally, the crow realized that he was soaring with the hawk the whole time. The hawk knew that the crow could not fly, but also, nobody took the time to see if he could not soar.
All of the spectators were watching in disbelief as the crow soared into the moonlit night sky along with the hawk.

That flock of crows must've learned their lessons, because every now and then, the crow Homie would be seen taking his morning walk down on the block with the hawk not too far away, screeching and soaring in the air, watching over the crow.

The END